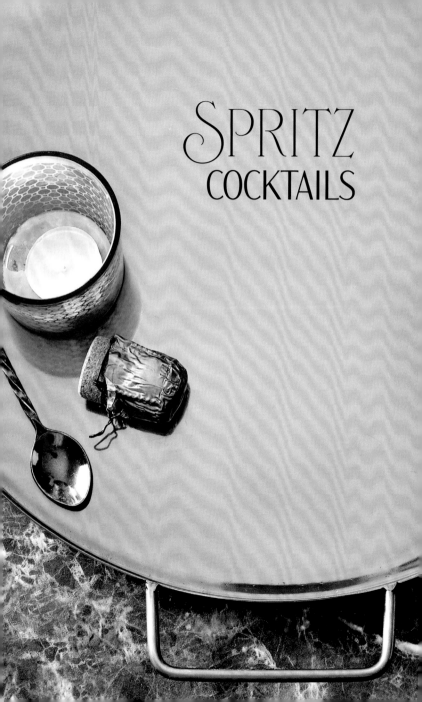

SPRITZ
COCKTAILS

SPRITZ
COCKTAILS

35 THIRST-QUENCHING SODAS, HIGHBALLS & SPARKLERS

photography by
Alex Luck

RYLAND PETERS & SMALL
LONDON • NEW YORK

Senior designer Toni Kay
Production manager
  Gordana Simakovic
Editorial director Julia Charles
Creative director Leslie Harrington
Food stylists Lorna Brash & Tara Garnell
Prop stylist Luis Peral
Indexer Vanessa Bird

First published in 2024 by
Ryland Peters & Small
20-21 Jockey's Fields
London WC1R 4BW
and
341 E 116th Street
New York, 10029

www.rylandpeters.com

10 9 8 7 6 5 4 3 2 1

Recipe collection compiled by
Julia Charles. Text © Julia Charles,
Jesse Estes, Laura Gladwin, David
T. Smith & Keli Rivers & Ryland Peters
& Small 2024. See page 64 for full
credits. Design and photography
© Ryland Peters & Small 2024.

ISBN: 978-1-78879-606-4

A CIP record for this book is available
from the British Library. US Library of
Congress CIP data has been applied for.

Printed in China

MIX
Paper | Supporting
responsible forestry
FSC
www.fsc.org   **FSC® C008047**

CONTENTS

Introduction   6

CLASSIC   8

CONTEMPORARY   22

EXPERIMENTAL   36

CELEBRATORY   52

Index and
Credits   64

INTRODUCTION

Spritz cocktails have become a popular choice for anyone seeking a refreshing and vibrant drinking experience.

Originating from Northern Italy, these fizzy concoctions typically combine sparkling wine, such as Prosecco, with a bitter Italian 'amaro' such as Aperol, Campari or Cynar, finished off with a splash of soda water and served long over ice. The result is a drink that effortlessly combines effervescence, bitterness and zestiness in each delicious sip.

While the original recipe for the Aperol Spritz remains beloved and enduring (see page 9), mixologists have now put their own spin on this style of cocktail, experimenting with different variations from tangy citrus-based spritzes to fruity and floral combinations, from refreshing herbal concoctions to enticing twists on classic cocktails, creating an endless array of options to suit every taste preference.

Making a spritz cocktail at home is easier than you may think. Here you will find recipes to inspire and delight, from Italian classics such as the Sbagliato (see page 14), to contemporary creations like the Prosecco Iced Tea (see page 27), from experimental twists like the Porch-Drinking Negroni (see page 46) and Japanese-inspired White Soy & Watermelon Spritz (see page 50) to celebratory delights including the Just Peachy Punch (see page 57) and Tutti Frutti Summer Sangria.

Whether you are mixing a cocktail for one or creating pitchers for a party, this collection of 35 inventive and sippable creations is sure to spritz up your drinking repertoire.

CLASSIC

THE PERFECT SPRITZ

Ignore what it says on the label of your Aperol bottle and make your spritz this way instead. The Italians knew what they were doing when they came up with this recipe.

35 ml/1½ oz Aperol
75 ml/3 oz well-chilled Prosecco
soda water, to top
slice of orange, to garnish

SERVES 1

Half-fill a large wine glass or collins glass with ice cubes. Pour in the Aperol and half the Prosecco and stir gently. Add the rest of the Prosecco, top with a splash of soda and add the orange slice. Serve immediately.

Hugo

Who's Hugo? His identity remains a mystery, but he came up with a damn fine drink. Let's imagine he's a suave, chisel-jawed man-about town who created this ravishing elderflower concoction just for you...

6 mint leaves
¼ lime, cut into wedges
25 ml/1 oz elderflower cordial
well-chilled Prosecco, to top
splash of soda water

SERVES 1

Put four of the mint leaves and the lime wedges in a balloon glass and muddle lightly. Add the elderflower cordial and a handful of ice cubes. Half-fill with Prosecco and stir gently. Top up with Prosecco and a splash of soda water and garnish with the remaining mint leaves. Serve with a straw.

Nonna's Garden

The gorgeous combination of cucumber and mint smells fresh and light – just like the beautiful garden an Italian nonna might spend her time tending! You can also try fresh basil or sage leaves instead of the mint.

3 large slices of cucumber,
   plus 1 small slice to garnish
1 teaspoon freshly squeezed
   lemon juice
1 teaspoon sugar
5 mint leaves
well-chilled Prosecco, to top

SERVES 1

Put the cucumber, lemon juice, sugar and four of the mint leaves into a cocktail shaker and muddle well. Half-fill the shaker with ice cubes and shake vigorously. Strain into a chilled balloon glass and top with Prosecco. Garnish with a mint leaf and a slice of cucumber.

LA PASSEGGIATA

The *passeggiata* is an excellent Italian tradition of taking an evening stroll along a scenic boulevard, dressed up to the nines, to check out your neighbours. Why not give it a try in your own neighbourhood, accompanied by one of these?

75 ml/3 oz chilled pink grapefruit juice
20 ml/¾ oz gin
20 ml/¾ oz Aperol
well-chilled Prosecco, to top
strip of grapefruit zest, to garnish
   (optional)

SERVES 1

Half-fill a collins glass with ice cubes. Add the pink grapefruit juice, gin and Aperol and stir well. Top with Prosecco and stir very briefly. If you like, squeeze a strip of grapefruit zest over the top and drop it in.

Sbagliato

No need to worry about your hand 'slipping' with the gin here –
sbagliato means 'mistaken', and this is a rough-and-ready,
but rather delicious version, of the iconic Negroni cocktail.

25 ml/1 oz red Italian vermouth
25 ml/1 oz Campari
75 ml/3 oz well-chilled Prosecco

SERVES 1

Fill an old-fashioned glass with ice
and add the vermouth and Campari.
Stir well. Add the Prosecco and stir
very gently to preserve the fizz.
Serve immediately.

Tiziano

This gorgeous red concoction would be just perfect to
kick off an intimate meal à deux. Dubonnet's Rouge Aperitif
wine has been a staple on the cocktail scene since
1846, and rightly so!

10 red grapes
75 ml/3 oz Dubonnet
well-chilled Prosecco, to top
strip of orange zest, to garnish

SERVES 1

Put nine of the grapes into a cocktail
shaker and muddle them to crush
and extract the juice. Add a handful
of ice cubes and the Dubonnet and
shake vigorously. Strain into an
old-fashioned glass, add some ice
and top with Prosecco. Squeeze
the zest lengthways to spritz the
essential oils in the orange peel over
the drink. Garnish with it and the
remaining grape on a cocktail stick.

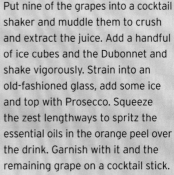

NEGRONI BIANCO BERGAMOTTO

Italy is the home of the Negroni and this variation includes a few extra ingredients from the *bel paese*. The Italicus Rosolio di Bergamotto liqueur not only comes in a bottle that is itself a work of art, but it is flavoured with botanicals such as yellow rose, gentian, chamomile and bergamot orange. The sparkling Prosecco adds a bright zing and liveliness to this drink.

25 ml/¾ oz gin
25 ml/¾ oz Suze
25 ml/¾ oz Dolin Bianco
25 ml/¾ oz Italicus Rosolio
   di Bergamotto Liqueur
well-chilled Prosecco, to top
slice of orange, to garnish

SERVES 1

Add the ingredients (except the Prosecco) to a large, ice-filled wine glass and gently stir. Top up with chilled Prosecco and garnish with an orange slice to serve.

Bar Note The peel of the bergamot orange used in Italicus Rosolio di Bergamotto Liqueur is most commonly associated with Earl Grey Tea, while the gentian is the key ingredient in Suze, a complex and slightly bittersweet liqueur.

Rosé Aperol Spritz

Bitter-sweet Aperol has seen a massive rise in popularity since its signature serve – the Aperol spritz – took the international bar scene by storm. This recipe peps it up further with the addition of sparkling rosé Prosecco, fragrant passion fruit juice and a hint of zesty lime.

50 ml/1¾ oz Aperol

25 ml/¾ oz passion fruit juice (such as Rubicon)

1 teaspoon freshly squeezed lime juice

75 ml/2½ oz well-chilled rosé Prosecco

lime wedges, to serve

SERVES 1

Fill a large balloon glass with ice cubes. Pour in the Aperol, passion fruit juice and lime juice. Stir with a barspoon and top up with cold rosé Prosecco. Garnish with a couple of wedges of lime and serve at once with a straw.

Strawberry Rosé Spritzer

A gentler version of the classic Aperol spritz that is deliciously light, fresh and fruity with an enticing strawberry scent. Serve as a summer aperitif.

15 ml/½ oz strawberry syrup

50 ml/1¾ oz Aperol

75 ml/2½ oz well-chilled fruity rosé wine (a Chilean Cabernet-based blend works well here)

15 ml/½ oz freshly squeezed lemon juice

about 200 ml/¾–1 cup soda water

strawberries and lemon slices, to garnish

SERVES 1

Pour the strawberry syrup into a highball glass or balloon glass. Add the Aperol, rosé wine and lemon juice and stir. Add plenty of ice cubes and top with up with soda water to taste, but no more than 200 ml/¾–1 cup. Garnish with sliced strawberries and lemon slices. Serve at once.

Sanguinello Fizz

This sophisticated sparkler celebrates all the sweet, tart
and bitter qualities of vibrant blood oranges, and will transport
you to a fragrant Sicilian orange grove in no time.

40 ml/1¾ oz blood orange juice
5 ml/1 teaspoon Campari
10 ml/⅓ oz limoncello
well-chilled Prosecco or other dry
    sparkling wine, to top
blood orange wheel, to garnish

SERVES 1

Pour the first three ingredients
into an ice-filled cocktail shaker
and shake well. Strain into a
chilled Champagne flute and top
with Prosecco. Garnish with a
blood orange wheel and serve.

CONTEMPORARY

NEWBIE NEGRONI

For many, the Negroni has the perfect combination of bitter and sweet complexity, but for drinkers coming across the cocktail for the first time, its intensity and bitterness can be overwhelming. This recipe has been designed to be a gentler introduction as it's served as a long spritz. The drink is both less sweet and less bitter thanks to the use of Pimms No. 1 in place of Campari and it will work with any dry gin or even, if you prefer, a fruitier style of gin.

25 ml/1 oz gin
25 ml/1 oz Sacred Rosehip Cup (or Pimm's No. 1)
25 ml/1 oz Italian red vermouth, such as Martini Rosso
15 ml/½ oz orange juice
25 ml/1 oz soda water, or more to taste
strips of lemon, lime and orange peel, to garnish

SERVES 1

Add the ingredients to a large ice-filled wine glass and top up with chilled soda water. If the drink is still too strong, add more soda water. Garnish with lemon, lime and orange peels to serve.

High-Rise Martini

Martinis are often short and potent, but on a hot summer's day it can be nice to have the taste of a martini in a spritz-style drink that is more refreshing and thirst-quenching.

30 ml/1 oz gin or vodka

1 barspoon dry vermouth

1 barspoon Bianco Vermouth

100 ml/3¼ oz sparkling water or sparkling lemonade

strips of lemon, lime and orange peel, to garnish

SERVES 1

Add the alcohols to an ice-filled highball glass (spirit first) and give the drink a gentle stir. Top up with sparkling water or lemonade and garnish with strips of lemon, lime and orange peel.

Prosecco Iced Tea

Tea, gin and Prosecco: all your favourite refreshments in one glass! Next time you fancy a Long Island Iced Tea, think again, and try this far more elegant concoction instead.

1 Earl Grey teabag
1 tablespoon sugar
25 ml/1 oz gin
1 teaspoon freshly squeezed
   lemon juice
dash of elderflower cordial
well-chilled Prosecco, to top
lemon slices, to garnish

SERVES 1

First, make an infusion by putting the teabag and sugar in a mug and pouring over 75 ml/3 oz boiling water, then leave for 5 minutes. Remove the teabag and leave to cool to room temperature.

Pour the Earl Grey infusion into a collins glass and add the gin, lemon juice and elderflower cordial. Half-fill with ice cubes and stir well. Top with Prosecco and garnish with a couple of lemon slices, and a straw if you like.

B&B

Strawberries and basil are one of nature's little flavour-pairing miracles, so bringing them together in a glass of rosé fizz that's already bursting with berry notes is a treat.

a mix of small strawberries (hulled), blackberries, raspberries and blueberries

15 ml/½ oz basil syrup (try Monin)

10 ml/¼ oz freshly squeezed lemon juice

200 ml/¾–1 cup sparkling rosé wine (a Cava Rosado works well here)

basil leaves and berries, to garnish

SERVES 1

First pop a berry into each compartment of an ice-cube tray. Top up with filtered water and put in the freezer until frozen solid.

Pour the basil syrup into a large wine glass. Add the lemon juice and top up with the cava. Add 4–5 berry-filled ice cubes to the glass. Garnish with a basil sprig and a few fresh berries and serve at once.

Blooming Lovely

Orange blossom extract has an indefinable flavour that isn't exactly floral, so it adds an intriguing taste to this elegant spritzer.

4 dashes of Peychaud's bitters

15 ml/½ oz St-Germain elderflower liqueur

¼ teaspoon orange blossom extract

½ teaspoon sugar syrup

120 ml/4 oz dry sparkling rosé, well chilled (a pink Champagne works well here)

2 lemon zests

edible flowers, to garnish

SERVES 1

Pour the bitters, elderflower liqueur, orange blossom extract and sugar syrup into a white wine glass and add a few ice cubes. Top up with Champagne, squeeze the lemon zests over the drink and discard. Stir, garnish with an edible flower and serve at once.

SUNSHINE NEGRONI

This, the Negroni's answer to a Tequila Sunrise
is just as visually stunning.

25 ml/¾ oz citrus-forward gin,
  such as Gordon's Sicilian Lemon Gin
25 ml/¾ oz Aperol
25 ml/¾ oz Dolin Bianco
10 ml/½ oz orange juice
35 ml/1 oz grapefruit soda
5 ml/¼ oz grenadine
slices of orange, to garnish

SERVES 1

Add the gin, Aperol, vermouth and orange juice
to an ice-filled highball glass and gently stir.
Top up with chilled grapefruit soda and slowly
pour the grenadine down the inside of the glass.
Garnish with orange slices to serve.

Bar Note Any grapefruit soda can be used here,
even something like Lilt, but for the optimal
visual effect it's best to use a white grapefruit
soda such as Ting or San Pellegrino over
a ruby or red grapefruit variety.

Spanish Strawberry

In 2015 a new alcohol phenomenon arrived in Spain: strawberry gin. Such was the popularity of this product in its birthplace of Valencia that within months, many more brands had entered the market. In Valencia, the Strawberry 'Gin Tonica' is not actually made by pairing the gin with tonic water, but rather Lemon Fanta, a slightly tart soft drink. The result is a lightly cloudy drink with a pinkish hue; the garnishes add visual brightness. The Lemon Fanta makes the drink sweeter than a normal Gin Tonica, so the use of slightly drier Blackwater Strawberry Gin gives the drink balance (another good choice would be Poetic License Strawberries and Cream Picnic Gin). For a tarter drink, try substituting the Lemon Fanta for bitter lemon.

50 ml/1¾ oz strawberry gin

120 ml/4 oz Lemon Fanta

fresh or frozen strawberries, quartered, and curled lemon peel, to garnish

SERVES 1

Add ice cubes to three-quarters fill a balloon glass. Stir gently for 15 seconds with a barspoon to chill the glass. Pour away any liquid from the melted ice, then top up the glass with more ice cubes. Add the gin, trying to ensure you coat the ice as you pour. Add the Lemon Fanta, add the strawberries and the lemon peel, then let the drink rest for 30 seconds to allow the flavours to integrate. Serve with a straw.

PROSECCO MARY

Think of this Prosecco Mary as the traditional
Bloody Mary's younger, more contemporary and
slightly more glamorous and 'spritzy' sister!

25 ml/1 oz vodka

75 ml/3 oz tomato juice

dash of Tabasco or sriracha sauce

pinch of sugar

dash of smoked water (optional; available
   in some supermarkets)

about 75 ml/3 oz Prosecco

cucumber slices and/or a celery stick/rib, to garnish

SERVES 1

Put the vodka, tomato juice, Tabasco, sugar and
smoked water, if using, into a cocktail shaker half-
filled with ice cubes. Shake vigorously and pour,
ice cubes and all, into a chilled collins glass. Add
half the Prosecco and stir gently to combine. Top
with the rest of the Prosecco, add some cucumber
slices down the side of the glass (or a celery stick/
rib if you prefer) and serve with straw and stirrer.

Bar Note Smoked water is delicious but can
overpower, so exercise caution and use
no more than 1/4 teaspoon to begin with.

EXPERIMENTAL

SPARKLING MANHATTAN

If you love Manhattans but sometimes find them a bit much, you'll love this. This is based on a Sweet Manhattan, but feel free to switch the sweet vermouth for dry if you prefer yours dry – or use half sweet and half dry vermouth if you're more of a Perfect Manhattan fan.

15 ml/½ oz bourbon
10 ml/⅓ oz Italian sweet red vermouth
dash of Angostura bitters
5 ml/1 teaspoon Maraschino,
    such as Luxardo (optional)
well-chilled Champagne or other
    dry sparkling wine, to top
maraschino cherries, to garnish

SERVES 1

Pour the first four ingredients into an ice-filled cocktail shaker and stir well. Strain into a chilled old-fashioned glass and top with Champagne. Garnish with maraschino cherries.

The Hartley

This is technically a refreshing gin and tonic rather than a spritz but it borrows a key ingredient from the Italian classic spritz, that is to say Campari. It needs a solid, classic gin as its base in order to stand up to the bittersweet flavours of the Campari, and makes a deliciously refreshing twist on the much-loved drink.

50 ml/1¾ oz gin

150 ml/5 oz Franklin & Sons Indian
   Tonic Water, or similar

5 ml/1 teaspoon fresh orange juice

5 ml/1 teaspoon Campari

slice of orange on a cocktail stick,
   to garnish

SERVES 1

Add ice, gin and tonic to a balloon glass, then add the orange juice, followed by the Campari. Finally, add the garnish.

Bar Note Good choices of gin include Loch Ness Gin, Sipsmith, Tanqueray, Hayman's London Dry Gin, Puddingstone Campfire Gin and Conker Spirit Dorset Dry Gin.

BELLO MARCELLO

Even the most committed whisky-phobe
will love this one. Surely there's no better use for
that dusty bottle at the back of the drinks cabinet!

35 ml/1½ oz whisky
15 ml/½ oz Cointreau
well-chilled Prosecco, to top
strip of lemon zest, to garnish

SERVES 1

Pour the whisky and Cointreau into an
old-fashioned glass filled with ice. Stir
well, then top up with Prosecco. Squeeze
the lemon zest in half lengthways over
the drink so that the essential oils in the
skin spritz over it, then add the zest to
the drink and serve.

AIRMAIL

Imagine you're sitting in the cocktail lounge on a luxury cruise liner, wearing vintage Dior and white satin gloves. This is almost certainly what you're drinking...

35 ml/1½ oz dark rum

15 ml/½ oz freshly squeezed lime juice

slice of lime

10 ml/¼ oz honey, mixed with 1 teaspoon boiling water

well-chilled Prosecco, to top

SERVES 1

Put the rum, lime juice and slice and honey in an old-fashioned glass, add a handful of ice cubes and stir. Top up with Prosecco and serve.

PROSECCO MOJITO

Everything you love about the mojito, with a dash of Prosecco in the mix instead of soda water to liven up proceedings.

10 mint leaves, plus extra to garnish

1 teaspoon sugar

½ lime, cut into wedges

35 ml/1½ oz white rum

well-chilled Prosecco, to top

SERVES 1

Put the mint leaves, sugar and lime wedges in a collins glass and muddle well. Add the rum, stir and fill the glass with crushed ice. Top with Prosecco and stir very gently. Serve with more lightly crushed mint leaves.

Prima Donna

Simply combine a zesty Italian lemon liqueur with vodka, tangy pomegranate juice and chilled Italian sparkling wine, for an elegant and pretty drink.

25 ml/¾ oz vodka
15 ml/½ oz Limoncello
   (Italian lemon liqueur)
25 ml/¾ oz pomegranate juice
chilled Prosecco, to top up
pomegranate seeds (optional) and
   orange slices, to garnish

SERVES 1

Put the vodka, limoncello and pomegranate juice in a cocktail shaker and add a handful of ice cubes. Shake sharply and strain into an ice-filled rocks glass or tumbler. Top up with Prosecco, garnish with pomegranate seeds and orange slices and serve.

Porch–Drinking Negroni

This laidback drink was just made for sipping on warm summer evenings. The muddled strawberries give it a soft, fruity note whilst the bitter lemon adds a refreshing crispness. You can use a soft, sippable gin, or something more intense and piney, as preferred.

3 strawberries
15 ml/¾ oz gin, your choice of style
10 ml/¾ oz Campari
10 ml/½ oz bianco vermouth
150 ml/5 oz bitter lemon
mint sprig, to garnish

SERVES 1

Muddle or crush the strawberries in the bottom of a rocks glass, then add the other ingredients and gently stir. Add ice and garnish with a mint sprig to serve.

The Negroni Cup

A longer version of the Porch-Drinking Negroni, this can be served by the pitcher so is ideal for gatherings.

75 ml/2½ oz gin
25 ml/1 oz sweet red vermouth
25 ml/1 oz ginger wine
25 ml/1 oz Campari
450 ml/15 oz sparkling lemonade
lemon wheels and cucumber slices, to garnish

SERVES 4

Combine the ingredients (except the lemonade) in a large jug/pitcher with ice and stir before garnishing with lemon wheels and cucumber slices. Top up with chilled lemonade and pour into ice-filled tumblers to serve.

WHISKY HIGHBALL

Japanese whisky is a relative newcomer to the scene, but has been making a big splash of late, becoming trendy in bars around Europe and North America and commanding high price tags for bottlings. The highball is believed by many to be the best way to enjoy Japanese whisky (along with drinking it neat or with water). Although on paper it looks simple, making the perfect highball in Japan is akin to an art form, with each bar having its own subtly different technique.

60 ml/2 oz Nikka Taketsuru
   Pure Malt Whisky, or other Japanese whisky

soda water, to top

lemon and/or orange zest or fresh mint
   sprig (optional), to garnish

SERVES 1

Fill a highball glass with large, clear ice cubes and carefully pour the whisky down the side of the glass so that it does not touch the top of the ice. Add the soda slowly in the same manner and stop filling once the soda reaches around 1 cm/$\frac{1}{3}$ inch from the top of the glass. Use a barspoon to mix the whisky and soda by placing the spoon between the ice and glass and moving the spoon up and down or in a circular motion for about 5–10 seconds. Serve without a straw. Garnish with citrus zest or a mint sprig to add aroma to the drink.

White Soy & Watermelon Spritz

Refreshing watermelon works incredibly well with salty flavours, and here it is paired with the earthy umami notes of white soy sauce to give a complex and moreish drink. White soy sauce is slightly milder than regular soy sauce, and is available in Japanese stores or online.

2.5 ml/½ teaspoon white soy sauce
10 ml/2 teaspoons sugar syrup
25 ml/¾ oz watermelon juice
25 ml/¾ oz vodka
chilled soda water, to top
fresh watermelon, to garnish

SERVES 1

Pour the white soy sauce, sugar syrup, watermelon juice and vodka into a highball glass over cubed ice. Stir to combine the ingredients, then top up with chilled soda water. Garnish with a small slice of watermelon and serve at once.

CELEBRATORY

PIMM'S DELUXE

Once you've tried this you'll wonder why you haven't been adding Prosecco to Pimm's all your life – it's a knockout (although it is best to keep in mind that it packs more of a punch than your regular Pimm's and lemonade!).

50 ml/2 oz Pimm's No. 1
dash of elderflower cordial
sliced strawberries, orange,
    lemon and cucumber
well-chilled Prosecco, to top
a sprig of mint

SERVES 1

Fill a collins glass with ice cubes and add the Pimm's, elderflower and sliced fruit. Stir well, then half-fill with Prosecco. Stir gently, then add the rest of the Prosecco. Lightly crush the mint sprig and drop it in the top.

Bar Note If serving lots of people, make a pitcher of this ahead of time, which helps extract more flavour from the fruit, adding the ice, Prosecco and mint just before serving. For a 2-litre/2-quart pitcher, use 750 ml/25 oz Prosecco, 400 ml/14 oz Pimms and 50 ml/2 oz elderflower cordial.

Spanish Fruit Cup

Here is a fresh take on a classic red-wine sangria. Fruity and citrusy, this is a deliciously thirst-quenching spritz to serve at a summer party or beach barbecue.

100 ml/3⅓ oz well-chilled fruity rosé wine
(a Spanish Garnacha works well here)
50 ml/1¾ oz smooth fresh orange juice
10 ml/¼ oz Spanish brandy
10 ml/¼ oz Cointreau (or other orange-flavoured liqueur)
200 ml/¾–1 cup Fever-Tree Mediterranean tonic water
(or any unflavoured tonic water if Fever-Tree not available)
orange and lemon wheels and green apple slices
a fresh strawberry, to garnish

SERVES 1

Pour all of the ingredients, the tonic last, into a large ice-filled balloon/copa glass and stir gently with a barspoon. Add a selection of the fruit slices. Garnish the rim of the glass with a strawberry slice. Serve at once.

Bar Note This also makes a wonderful pitcher drink, so simply use a 750-ml/25-oz bottle of rosé and multiply the other ingredients by 7 to serve 6–8 people.

JUST PEACHY PUNCH

A pale pink Provençal rosé, peach purée and French brandy enjoy a ménage à trois here with delicious results. Ooh là là!

4 ripe peaches, stoned/pitted and cut into wedges

75 ml/2½ oz French brandy

75 ml/2½ oz peach schnapps

1 x 750-ml/25-oz bottle well-chilled light, crisp rosé (a Provençal style works well here)

375 ml/1½ cups bottled French peach juice/nectar or purée (see Bar Note)

1-1½ litres/4-6 cups well-chilled Indian tonic water

peach slices and fresh basil sprigs, to garnish

SERVES 6–8

Put the peaches in a large jug/pitcher, pour over the brandy and schnapps and leave to marinate for a few hours.

When ready to serve, pour the wine into the jug/pitcher along with the peach juice/nectar and add plenty of ice cubes. Stir and top up to taste with tonic. Pour into ice-cube-filled tumblers, garnish each serving with a peach slice and a sprig of basil and serve at once.

Bar Note If you can't find bottled peach juice or purée, blend about 6 stoned/pitted ripe peaches (to yield 375 ml/1½ cups of juice) and pass the purée through a sieve/strainer to remove any fibre or lumps. Taste and sweeten to taste if necessary with a little sugar syrup before using – this will depend on the ripeness of the peaches used.

Spicy Ginger & Berry Cooler

Here is a super-simple spritz that requires the minimum of effort but tastes delicious nonetheless, whilst being lower in alcohol than many pitcher recipes as it contains no spirits. It needs to sit in the fridge overnight to allow the fruit to macerate in the wine and add flavour. The hint of spice from the ginger ale adds the finishing touch.

1 x 750-ml/25-oz bottle fruity, sweet rosé wine
(an Italian Montepulciano works well here)

100 g/1 cup strawberries, hulled and sliced,
plus extra to serve

100 g/1 cup raspberries

50 g/¼ cup white caster/granulated sugar

1 litre/4 cups well-chilled sparkling ginger ale

1 orange, thinly sliced, to garnish

SERVES 6–8

Pour the wine into a large jug/pitcher and add the strawberries, raspberries and sugar. Cover and marinate overnight in the fridge.

When ready to serve, pour the ginger ale into the jug/pitcher and stir. Add ice cubes and pour into ice-cube-filled tumblers. Add a few berries to each serving and garnish with orange slices. Serve at once.

CHERRY VANILLA KISS

A sparkling treat for those with a passion for all things cherry.

125 ml/½ cup white sugar

400 g/2 cups fresh sweet cherries, stoned/pitted

1 vanilla pod/bean, whole

1 x 750-ml/25-oz bottle bold, fruity rosé wine (an Australian Shiraz works well)

125 ml/½ cup brandy

125 ml/½ cup Morello cherry cordial

65 ml/¼ cup cherry bitters (or Peychaud's or Angostura bitters)

500 ml/2 cups soda water, chilled

8 vanilla pods/beans, to garnish

SERVES 8

Bring 125 ml/½ cup water and the sugar to a simmer in a small saucepan, and stir until the sugar has just dissolved. Remove from the heat. Put the cherries and vanilla pod/bean into a large jug/pitcher, pour in the warm syrup and let stand for 5 minutes.

Add the wine, brandy, cherry cordial and cherry bitters and stir to combine. Chill for at least 1 hour. When ready to serve, add the soda and pour into ice-cube-filled highball glasses. Garnish each serving with a vanilla pod/bean and serve at once.

TUTTI FRUTTI SUMMER SANGRIA

Deliciously pretty – full of juicy fruit and pink ice cubes.

2 x 750-ml/25-oz bottles well-chilled dark, fruity, very sweet sparkling rosé wine (a Californian Zinfandel works well)

8 sweet cherries, pitted and halved

8 strawberries, hulled and sliced

1–2 white peaches, pitted and sliced

freshly squeezed juice of 1 lime

6 sugar cubes

225 ml/8 oz vodka

225 ml/1 cup fresh watermelon juice

fresh cherries and lime wedges, to garnish

SERVES 6

First make the rosé ice cubes. Pour 1 bottle of rosé into ice-cube trays and transfer to the freezer. Meanwhile, combine the other ingredients (apart from the second bottle of rosé) in a large jug/pitcher. Leave for at least 2 hours.

When ready to serve, add the ice cubes and the second bottle of rosé and stir. Pour into glasses, garnish with a cherry and a lime wedge and serve at once.

Sparkling
Mediterranean Punch

The scent of thyme in this punch will transport you to a
village nestled on a hilltop in Tuscany. This recipe makes
an extra-large quantity so it is ideal for an al-fresco party.
You'll need a 3.5-litre/scant 4 quart capacity punch
bowl or drinks dispenser to serve.

4 sprigs of fresh thyme, plus extra to garnish

1 x 750-ml/25-oz bottle Aperol, well chilled

1 x 750-ml/25-oz bottle dry white vermouth, well chilled
   (Lillet works well here)

1 litre/4 cups fresh pink or white grapefruit juice

1 x 750-ml/25-oz bottle well- chilled juicy, sparkling rosé wine
   (a Cava Rosada or rosé Prosecco both work well here)

slices of pink grapefruit, to garnish

SERVES 20

Combine the thyme sprigs, Aperol, vermouth
and grapefruit juice in a jug/pitcher and chill
forat least 2 hours.

Pour into a large punch bowl, add the sparkling
rosé and plenty of ice cubes. Add a few ice cubes
and a slice of grapefruit to each serving glass
(small wine glasses or tumblers can be used).
Pour in the punch and add a sprig of fresh thyme
wto each serving to garnish. Serve at once.

INDEX

A B
Airmail 42
B&B 28
Bello Marcello 41
Blooming Lovely 28

C
Cherry Vanilla Kiss 61
cooler: Spicy Ginger &
   Berry Cooler 58

H
the Hartley 38
High-Rise Martini 24
Highball: Whisky
   Highball 49
Hugo 10

I J
Iced Tea: Prosecco Iced
   Tea 27
Just Peachy Punch 57

L M
La Passeggiata 13

Manhattan: Sparkling
   Manhattan 37
Martini: High-Rise
   Martini 24
Mojito: Prosecco Mojito 42

N
Negroni
   Negroni Bianco
      Bergamotto 17
   the Negroni Cup 46
   Newbie Negroni 23
   Porch-Drinking
      Negroni 46
   Sunshine Negroni 31
Nonna's Garden 10

P
La Passeggiata 13
the Perfect Spritz 9
Pimm's Deluxe 53
Porch-Drinking Negroni 46
Prima Donna 45
Prosecco Iced Tea 27
Prosecco Mary 35
Prosecco Mojito 42
punches
   Just Peachy Punch 57

Sparkling Mediterranean
   Punch 62

R S
Rosé Aperol Spritz 18
Sangria: Tutti Frutti
   Summer Sangria 61
Sanguinello Fizz 21
Sbagliato 14
Spanish Fruit Cup 54
Spanish Strawberry 32
Sparkling Manhattan 37
Sparkling Mediterranean
   Punch 62
Spicy Ginger & Berry
   Cooler 58
Strawberry Rosé Spritzer 18
Sunshine Negroni 31

T
Tiziano 14
Tutti Frutti Summer
   Sangria 61

W
Whisky Highball 49
White Soy & Watermelon
   Spritz 50

RECIPE CREDITS

Julia Charles
B&B
Blooming Lovely
Cherry Vanilla Kiss
Just Peachy Punch
Rosé Aperol Spritz
Spanish Fruit Cup
Sparkling Mediterranean
   Punch
Spicy Ginger & Berry
   Cooler
Strawberry Rosé Spritzer
Tutti Frutti Summer
   Sangria

Leigh Clarke
White Soy & Watermelon
   Spritz

Jesse Estes
Whisky Highball

Laura Gladwin
Airmail
Bello Marcello
Hugo
La Passeggiata
Nonna's Garden
Pimm's Deluxe
Prima Donna
Prosecco Iced Tea
Prosecco Mary

Prosecco Mojito
Sanguinello Fizz
Sbagliato
Sparkling Manhattan
The Perfect Spritz
Tiziano

**David T. Smith
& Keli Rivers**
High Rise Martini
Negroni Bianco
Bergamotto
Newbie Negroni
Porch-drinking Negroni
Spanish Strawberry
Sunshine Negroni
The Hartley